YORK

A Brief History

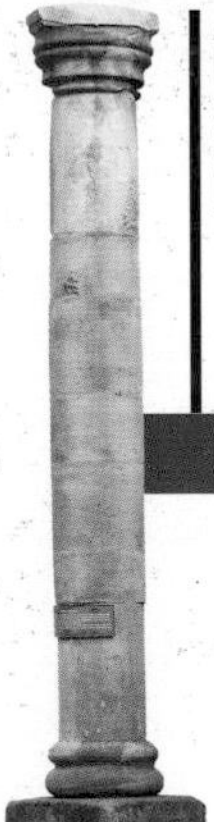

AD 71
Romans set up
military camp.
300
Multangular
Tower built.

306
Constantine
declared Emperor.
410
Romans withdraw.
627
Edwin marries
Ethelburga and is
baptised.

c.640
Oswald builds first
stone Minster.
866
Vikings capture city.
1068
William the
Conqueror destroys
York and builds castle.

1070
First Norman
Minster begun.
1088
St Mary's Abbey
founded. Many
religious houses
built.

1220–1472
Building of present Minster.
1328
Edward III married
Philippa of Hainault
in the Minster.
1400
Medieval York at height
of prosperity and power.

1461
St William's College founded.
1486
Marriage of Henry VII
and Elizabeth of York.
1536
Robert Aske, leader of
Pilgrimage of Grace,
executed in York.

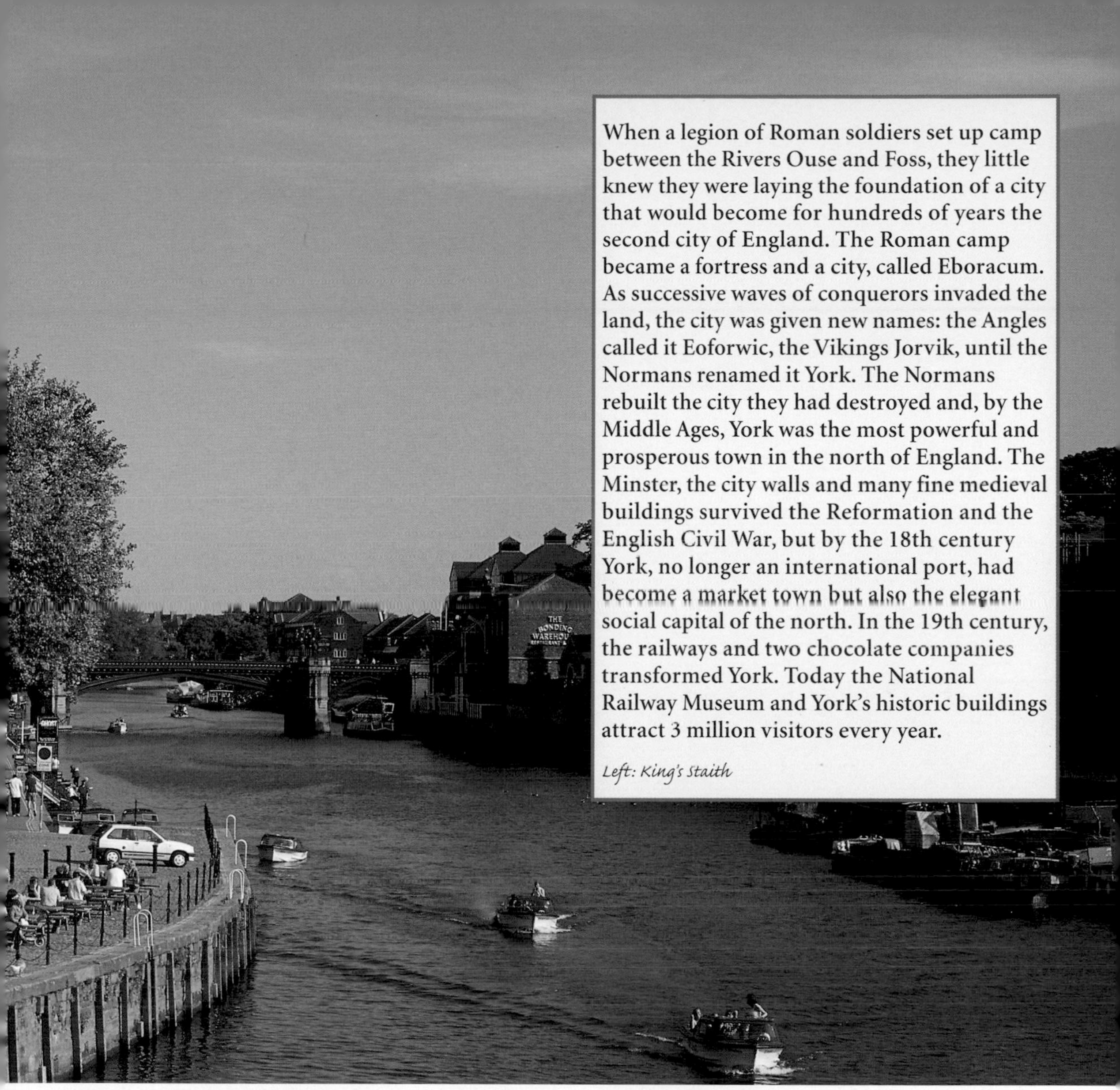

When a legion of Roman soldiers set up camp between the Rivers Ouse and Foss, they little knew they were laying the foundation of a city that would become for hundreds of years the second city of England. The Roman camp became a fortress and a city, called Eboracum. As successive waves of conquerors invaded the land, the city was given new names: the Angles called it Eoforwic, the Vikings Jorvik, until the Normans renamed it York. The Normans rebuilt the city they had destroyed and, by the Middle Ages, York was the most powerful and prosperous town in the north of England. The Minster, the city walls and many fine medieval buildings survived the Reformation and the English Civil War, but by the 18th century York, no longer an international port, had become a market town but also the elegant social capital of the north. In the 19th century, the railways and two chocolate companies transformed York. Today the National Railway Museum and York's historic buildings attract 3 million visitors every year.

Left: King's Staith

1539
St Mary's Abbey dissolved by Henry VIII.
1586
Margaret Clitheroe crushed to death.

1642
Charles I moves court to York.
1644
York besieged during English Civil War.

c.1725
York becomes social capital of northern England.
1732
Assembly Rooms opened.

1829
Jonathon Martin sets fire to the Minster.
1839
George Hudson brings railways to York.

1841
De Grey Rooms opened.
1860s
Rowntree and Terry expand chocolate business.

1968
Centre of York made a conservation area.
1984
Lightning causes fire in the Minster.

1990s
Excavation and reconstruction of Barley Hall.

York Minster

York Minster, the largest medieval Gothic church in northern Europe, dominates the city and is the chief church in the northern province of the Church of England. It is the fifth cathedral to be built on the site since Edwin, the Anglian king of Northumbria, was baptised here in 627. The current Minster is largely unchanged since it was completed in 1472, although it has suffered three fires in the last two centuries. The most recent, caused by lightning in 1984, destroyed the roof of the south transept.

Rose window

The nave

ROSE WINDOW

The stained glass of the rose window was designed soon after the end of the Wars of the Roses (▷ 9). The red and white roses around the central sunflower denote the union of the houses of York and Lancaster by the marriage of Henry VII to Elizabeth of York in 1486. The fire of 1984 melted the lead joints and cracked the glass, but the window survived intact. It was restored, and strengthened by sandwiching it between pieces of clear glass.

THE NAVE

The Minster has the widest Gothic nave in England. The high arches give an immense feeling of light, air and spirituality. The choir screen, carved with the kings of England from William I to Henry VI, divides the nave. In medieval times services were held in the choir and the vast open space of the nave was used for processions.

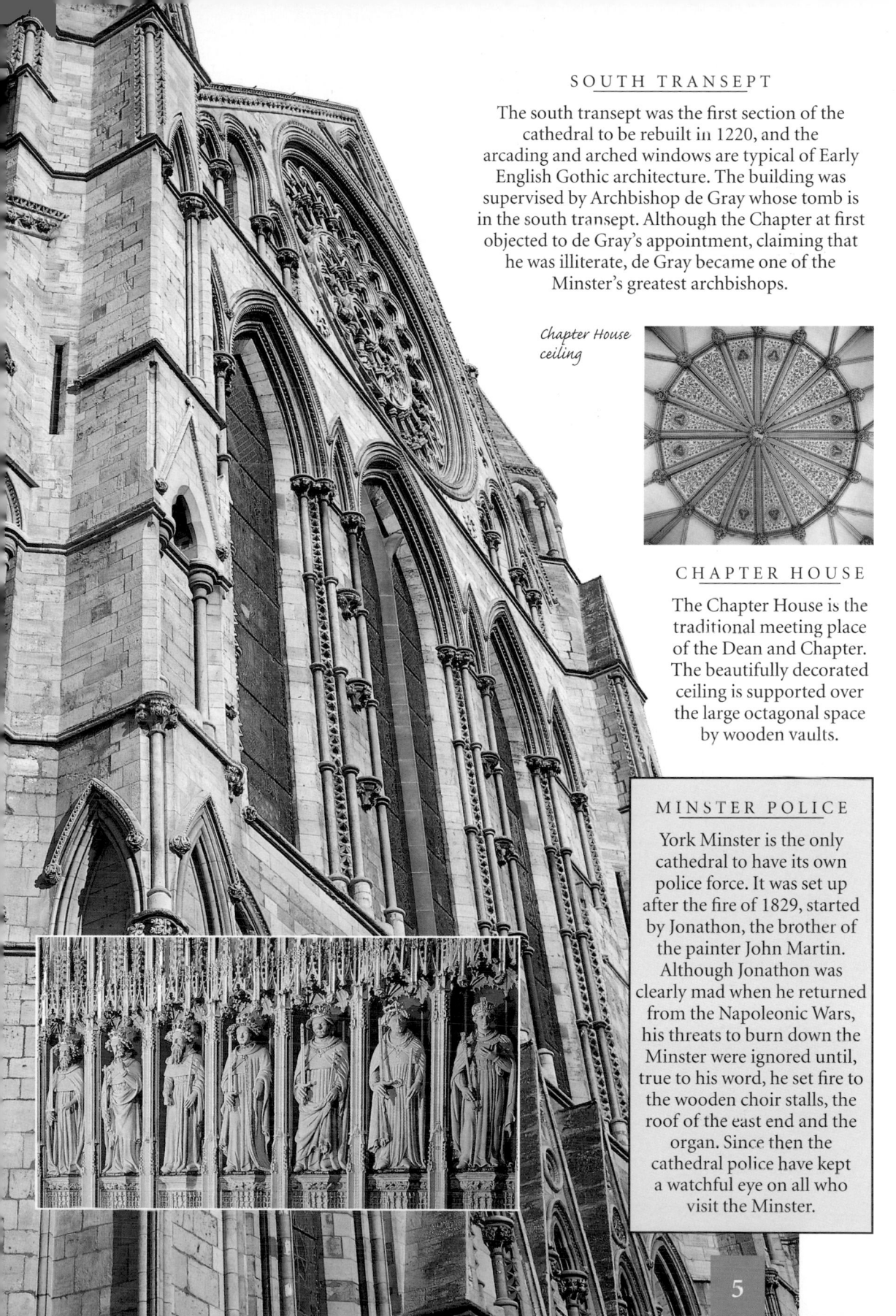

SOUTH TRANSEPT

The south transept was the first section of the cathedral to be rebuilt in 1220, and the arcading and arched windows are typical of Early English Gothic architecture. The building was supervised by Archbishop de Gray whose tomb is in the south transept. Although the Chapter at first objected to de Gray's appointment, claiming that he was illiterate, de Gray became one of the Minster's greatest archbishops.

Chapter House ceiling

CHAPTER HOUSE

The Chapter House is the traditional meeting place of the Dean and Chapter. The beautifully decorated ceiling is supported over the large octagonal space by wooden vaults.

MINSTER POLICE

York Minster is the only cathedral to have its own police force. It was set up after the fire of 1829, started by Jonathon, the brother of the painter John Martin. Although Jonathon was clearly mad when he returned from the Napoleonic Wars, his threats to burn down the Minster were ignored until, true to his word, he set fire to the wooden choir stalls, the roof of the east end and the organ. Since then the cathedral police have kept a watchful eye on all who visit the Minster.

Minster Precincts

The Minster is built over, and is surrounded by, history. Part of the foundations of the military headquarters of the Roman garrison and those of the first Norman Minster can still be seen in the crypt. Close to the Minster stand St William's College and the Treasurer's House.

Statue of Emperor Constantine

ROMAN COLUMN

This single column is the sole survivor of the 36 columns that supported a great hall in the Roman garrison. It was in this hall that Constantine was proclaimed Emperor.

Column from Roman great hall

EMPEROR CONSTANTINE (c.280–337)

When Emperor Constantius Chlorus died in York in 306, the troops proclaimed his son Constantine Emperor, but Constantine had to return to Rome to fight for the title. Six years later, Constantine, now Emperor, was baptised and by the end of the 4th century Christianity was the official religion of the Roman Empire.

WILLIAM FITZHERBERT

St William's College is dedicated to William Fitzherbert, a great-grandson of William the Conqueror. He was elected Archbishop of the Minster but then exiled by the Pope to Sicily. When the Pope died in 1153 he was re-elected Archbishop and was welcomed back to York by such a large, enthusiastic crowd of people that the bridge over the Ouse collapsed under their weight. Miraculously no one drowned, due, it was believed, to William's prayers. However within a month of his becoming Archbishop, William suddenly died, poisoned perhaps by a resentful archdeacon. Miracles were soon reported and in 1227 William was canonised.

ST WILLIAM'S COLLEGE

St William's College was founded in 1461 as a home for the chantry priests. In the late Middle Ages, many wealthy merchants endowed the Minster with a sum of money to hire a priest to say masses for their souls. The chantry priests were usually young and often high-spirited – St William's College was built close to the Minster to provide cheap lodgings where the priests could be kept under control.

TREASURER'S HOUSE

Until the Reformation, the Treasurer, who was responsible for the Minster's finances and treasures, lived in a house on this site. The present house was built at the end of the 17th century in an architectural style that includes Dutch gables in deference to the Dutch king William and his wife Mary who had been invited to take over the British throne. The house is now owned and run by The National Trust.

City Wall

The Romans surrounded their fortress with a strong wall, which was pulled down, expanded and rebuilt as successive invaders took over the city. The current wall was built between the 12th and 14th centuries to defend the medieval city. It is nearly three miles long and is the best-preserved city wall in Britain.

BOOTHAM BAR

Bootham Bar is the oldest gateway and stands on the site of the northern entrance to the Roman fortress. Some of the stonework on the gateway dates back to the 11th century, although most is later. In medieval times, guards were posted here to guide travellers through the dangerous Forest of Galtres to the north of the city.

MONK BAR

Monk Bar, one of four main gateways that breached the medieval city wall, still has a working portcullis. It is the most ornate of the surviving gateways, with carved figures on top of the towers poised to drop stones on the enemy below.

Bootham Bar in the 1880s

Monk Bar

Little Ease prison cell

RICHARD III MUSEUM

A narrow staircase leads from the street up to the museum, the portcullis and the wall. The museum features Richard III and the Wars of the Roses and includes Little Ease prison cell, used during the Reformation to imprison Roman Catholics who refused to become Protestants. The cell measures only 1.6 metres (5.5 feet) across and, unless you suffer from claustrophobia, you may like to try it out!

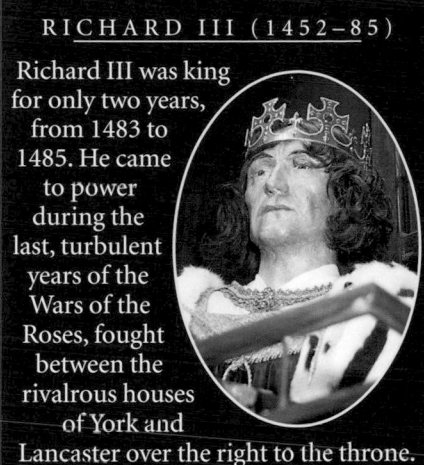

RICHARD III (1452–85)

Richard III was king for only two years, from 1483 to 1485. He came to power during the last, turbulent years of the Wars of the Roses, fought between the rivalrous houses of York and Lancaster over the right to the throne. Richard was suspected of being responsible for the murders of Edward V and his brother in 1483 and in his play, 'Richard III', Shakespeare portrays him as a villainous, hunchbacked tyrant, a reputation that clings to him still.

CITY WALL

The section of wall between Monk Bar and Bootham Bar is built over the site of the original Roman wall and the wide ditch on the outer side is the remains of the moat that once helped to protect the city. A walk along the wall gives excellent views of the Minster, Deanery Gardens and Dean's Park.

MINSTER LIBRARY

The Minster Library, which dates from the 13th century, was once the chapel of the Archbishop's Palace and is all that remains of it. It now holds the Minster's immense collection of books.

Dean's Park from the city wall

Stonegate

The area to the south of the Minster is filled with narrow medieval streets, often with Viking names, built over older streets. Stonegate and High Petergate follow the routes of Via Praetoria and Via Principalis – the two main roads across the Roman Garrison. Today they are crammed with small shops selling books, china, teddy bears and many other gifts.

STONEGATE

When you wander along Stonegate, look not only in the shop windows, but at the buildings too. Most of the façades are Georgian or Victorian, although the shops themselves are medieval in structure. Mulberry Hall is a beautifully preserved 15th-century building and Ye Old Starre Inn is said to be the oldest ale house in York. The Stonegate Devil, under the eaves of No. 33, shows that the building was once a printer's workshop.

NO. 10 STONEGATE

In the 19th century the front of this medieval house in Stonegate was covered with Minton tiles, to give a uniquely beautiful facade.

No. 10 Stonegate

Stonegate Devil

Stonegate

SNICKETS AND ALLEYWAYS

York's ancient streets are connected by narrow passageways, courts and back alleys. These shortcuts were muddy paths in medieval days and today their names reveal some of their history. You can, for example, still buy coffee in Coffee Yard.

Figurehead in Stonegate

BARLEY HALL

Barley Hall, the timber-framed house of William Snawsell, a 15th-century alderman, was discovered only recently among dilapidated buildings in Coffee Yard, just off Stonegate. The house is being restored and furnished as it was in 1483, not as a museum but as a place where you can peek inside chests, sit on the chairs and dress up in costumes of the time.

STATUE OF MINERVA

Minerva

Minerva, the Roman goddess of wisdom and knowledge, perches on the corner of High Petergate and Minster Gates and shows that the shop below was once a bookshop. In the days when few people could read, shop signs displayed visual symbols instead of names.

GUY FAWKES (1570–1606)

Guy Fawkes was born in York, baptised in St Michael-le-Belfrey and educated at St Peter's School. He later became famous for his part in a plot to blow up the Houses of Parliament in London. He was arrested, tortured and executed and, ever since, bonfires have been lit on 5 November and an effigy of Guy Fawkes burnt, but not at St Peter's School since the school does not burn 'old boys'!

The Shambles

The Shambles is York's most famous street and the only one mentioned in the Domesday Book of 1086. It is so narrow that, from the upper storeys of two of its timber-framed medieval buildings, people can shake hands across the street. For centuries butchers and slaughter-houses occupied the street.

THE SHAMBLES

A hundred years ago there were still 31 butchers in the Shambles. They laid out their meat on low, wide shelves (shammels) in front of the open windows. Today, gift shops have taken over the street and the last remaining butcher, in Little Shambles, displays his meat more hygienically.

HOLY TRINITY CHURCH

When you walk inside Holy Trinity, built between 1250 and 1500, the noise and bustle of the streets outside are at once forgotten. Boxed wooden pews fill the uneven floor of the nave and the side chapel retains its 'squint', a hole in the wall through which the priest could see the High Altar.

LADY ROW

Lady Row on Goodramgate is the oldest surviving row of houses in York. The cottages were built in 1316 by Thomas Langtoft, a wealthy merchant, so that their rent would pay for a chantry priest of the Virgin Mary in the church of Holy Trinity.

Golden Fleece, Pavement

The Shambles

PAVEMENT

Pavement, at the southern end of the Shambles, was first mentioned in 1329 and so was probably one of the first streets in York to be paved. The half-timbered building next to the Golden Fleece dates back to 1620 and belonged to a friend of Charles I, Sir Thomas Herbert, who kept the king company the night before his execution.

MARGARET CLITHEROE
(1556–1586)

Margaret Clitheroe, a butcher's wife, lived in the Shambles at a time when Roman Catholics were persecuted for their faith. She was arrested for celebrating mass and for hiding Jesuit priests in the attic of her home, and executed by having a wooden door, weighted with heavy stones, placed over her body until she was slowly crushed to death. In 1970 she was canonised and her house in the Shambles is now a shrine.

KING'S SQUARE

King's Square, built on the site of one of the gateways to the Roman fortress, was the graveyard of Christ Church until 1937. Some of the tombstones were used to pave the square. Today, you will almost always find buskers here and, on one of the rooftops, a stone cat poised to pounce on a stone pigeon.

Juggler in King's Square

Castle Gardens

The area around Clifford's Tower has played a part in York's history since 1068 when William the Conqueror built a castle and mound here. Clifford's Tower, built on the same mound 200 years later, was a garrison until the end of the 17th century. In the 18th century two prisons and the Court of Assizes were built on the old bailey area of the castle. The Court of Assizes remains, but the two prisons now house the Castle Museum, a unique evocation of everyday life in Yorkshire during the last 300 years.

19th-century fan

CASTLE MUSEUM

This Victorian street has been recreated in the Castle Museum. It is called Kirkgate after Dr John Kirk, a country doctor from Pickering, who in the first half of the 20th century began to collect Victorian and Edwardian everyday objects that were no longer used. His collection formed the basis of the Castle Museum, now the most popular folk museum in Britain. The Museum also includes prison cells, a gypsy caravan, jewellery and the detailed reconstruction of homes, shops and inns as they once were.

Kirkgate in the Castle Museum

Clifford's Tower

CLIFFORD'S TOWER

Clifford's Tower was built by Henry III between 1244 and 1270 on the site of a previous tower – the scene of an appalling Jewish massacre in 1190. This tower is the only remaining part of York Castle and is one of York's best-known landmarks. A walk around the top of the walls gives an excellent view of the city.

EYE OF YORK

Prisons in Castle Yard, 1841

The imposing buildings of the Castle Museum were built in the 18th century as a female prison and a debtors' prison, and were described by Daniel Defoe as 'the most stately and complete prison of any kind in the kingdom'. Conditions inside, however, were much less impressive! Dick Turpin, the notorious highwayman, was held here until he was hanged in 1739 on Knavesmire, near York. The Castle Museum was set up in the empty prison buildings in 1938.

ROBERT ASKE

Robert Aske led the Pilgrimage of Grace, an uprising of 30,000 northerners, against Henry VIII's Dissolution of the Monasteries. The king was so alarmed at the size of the protest, he offered the leaders an unlimited pardon and a parliament in York. Aske dismissed his followers but the king reneged on his promises. Aske and several other leaders were arrested and executed. Aske was hanged in chains from Clifford's Tower in 1537.

MERCHANT ADVENTURERS' HALL

Medieval York was an international port. Ships sailed down the River Ouse, laden with wool and cloth, and returned with goods from Europe and beyond. Each craft in this busy city had its own guild, and the Merchant Adventurers, who controlled the cloth trade, was the most powerful. The Hall with its hospital and chapel in the under-croft was built between 1357 and 1361 and is one of the best-preserved medieval guildhalls in Europe.

Jorvik Viking Festival

Every February York becomes a spectacle of colour and drama as the city celebrates the ancient Viking festival of Jolablot, which marked the coming of spring. Hordes of Vikings occupy the city and ranks of armed Viking warriors clash swords with Saxon soldiers in a re-enactment of the Viking invasion of York in 866. Other events include a race of Viking long-ships, a traditional Viking feast, ceilidh and dance, story-telling and demonstrations of traditional crafts with Viking horn-blowing, battle drills and a Viking fancy dress competition.

'Viking' warrior

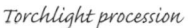
Torchlight procession

Re-enactment of Viking invasion

WHAT'S ON

Full and up-to-date information on all events is available from the Tourist Information Centre.

February	Jorvik Viking Festival
	Thomas the Tank Engine Week at
	the National Railway Museum
May	City of York Busking Festival
May-Oct	York Races
June	Lord Mayor's Parade
July	York Early Music Festival
August	Ebor Festival, York Racecourse
	Elvington Air Spectacular
September	York National Book Fair
	Festival of Food and Drink
St Nicholas Christmas Fayre:	
November	Christmas Lights Switch-on Show
December	French Christmas Market
	Pantomine in the Theatre Royal

York Mystery Plays

Every four years York stages the medieval Mystery Plays. These plays date back to the Middle Ages when every year, during the feast of Corpus Christi, the guilds performed a cycle of 48 plays which re-enacted the stories of the Bible from the Creation to the Last Judgement. Today the plays, which involve over 200 local actors and musicians, have lost none of their drama and power.

Viking long-ship finishes the long-ship race

Coppergate

York's past is preserved in its buildings and concealed under the streets, nowhere more so than in Coppergate. Under the modern shopping centre is an excavated and reconstructed Viking street – the Jorvik Viking Centre. Close by is Fairfax House, off Castlegate.

A Viking home in the 10th century

Dining-room in Fairfax House

JORVIK VIKING CENTRE

The refurbished Jorvik Viking Centre, opening in the spring, recreates life in Viking York, with a time capsule taking you back through the ages to the City of Jorvik in the 10th century. Modern-day technology breathes life into archaeological evidence, recreating the hustle and bustle of this important Viking trading port.

FAIRFAX HOUSE

Fairfax House is one of the finest 18th-century town houses in Britain. It was designed by John Carr in the 1760s for the 9th Viscount of Fairfax. Today the house has been refurnished in Georgian style, even including a sumptuous table-setting in the dining room. During December Christmas is recreated here as it was celebrated in the 18th century.

YORK DUNGEON

Deep in the heart of the city, beneath Clifford Street, lies York Dungeon, bringing the gruesome side of York's history vividly to life. Ghostly Roman soldiers, the highwayman Dick Turpin on the eve of his execution, and a grisly look at the effects of the Black Death, can all be seen.

Viking pendant

LITTLE TREATS IN YORK

- A Yorkshire 'Fat Rascal' bun at Betty's, the world-famous tearoom. (▷ 21)

- A teddy bear from one of the teddy bear shops in Stonegate. (▷ 10)

- A horse and carriage ride through the streets of York.

- Listening to ghost stories at Micklegate Bar Museum. (▷ 32)

- Listening to Evensong or, during August and September on Saturdays, an organ recital, in the Minster. (▷ 4)

- Views of the Minster from Dean's Park (▷ 9), or from the City wall between Bootham Bar and Monk Bar, or from the top floor of Marks & Spencer – a telescope is available!

- A river-boat cruise down the Ouse, especially at night. (▷ 22)

At work in the ARC

PARLIAMENT STREET

Parliament Street is a wide, open street, where traffic is banished during the day, allowing shoppers to relax, listen to buskers, or play street games of draughts and chess.

ARC

York's Archaeological Resource Centre is housed in a restored medieval church, St Saviour's, on St Saviourgate. Visitors can take on the role of archaeologists, finding out what lies below the streets of modern-day York, handling pottery, bones, leather and shells from Viking times and drawing conclusions about what life was like in the past. Opening times vary, so contact the centre in advance.

St Helen's Square

St Helen's Square throngs with people who converge here from five different streets. Many take advantage of the seats in the centre of the square to rest before continuing on their way. The square itself contains the church of St Helen and the Mansion House with the Guildhall behind.

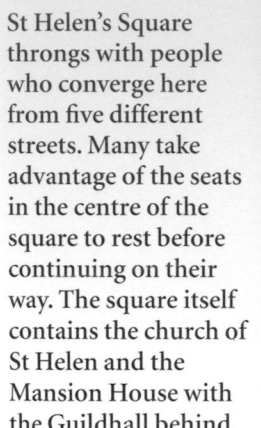

LITTLE ADMIRAL

The church of St Martin-le-Grand was flattened in a bombing raid in 1942, and partly rebuilt. The clock in Coney Street, which dates from 1778, has the face of Father Time on the side and a figure known as the Little Admiral on top. The admiral is using a cross-staff, a forerunner of the sextant, to calculate the altitude of the sun and his position of latitude.

MANSION HOUSE

The Mansion House is home to the Lord Mayor and is, therefore, not usually open to the public. It was built between 1725 and 1730 and probably designed by William Etty who helped Hawksmoor to design the mausoleum at Castle Howard. At the top of the façade, in the pediment, is the city's coat of arms.

YORK'S CHOCOLATE-MAKERS

Terry and Rowntree are two famous names in chocolate manufacture. Both were Quaker families who came to York in the 18th century, following the establishment of the Friends' Meeting House in Clifford Street in 1674. Terry's opened their business in St Helen's Square. Both companies provided jobs for hundreds of York people and the Rowntree family provided much more – schools, homes and a new social relationship between employer and employees, which contributed eventually to the founding of Britain's welfare state.

GUILDHALL

Hidden away down a narrow passage beside the Mansion House is the entrance to the Guildhall. This building dates from the 15th century when its hall was used as a meeting place for guilds and, in 1483, to entertain Richard III to a splendid feast. The Guildhall was bombed during the Second World War, and much of it subsequently rebuilt to the original designs. Today York City Council use the building for meetings, concerts and exhibitions.

Entrance to the Guildhall

BETTY'S

Now a world-famous teahouse, Betty's in St Helen's Square was a meeting place for locals and airmen during the war. The large mirror with the airmen's signatures is still hanging on the lower floor.

ST HELEN'S SQUARE

St Helen's Square was the site of the main gateway to the Roman fortress and then, until 1745, the graveyard to St Helen's Church. Some of the original gravestones can still be seen in a secluded niche on Davygate.

St Helen's Square

River Ouse

For centuries the River Ouse was the main route into and out of the city – ships sailed from the Humber and unloaded at King's Staith and Queen's Staith as recently as the 1880s. The Romans probably built the first bridge across the Ouse on the site of the present Ouse Bridge. It was not until the middle of the 19th century, when rail travel came to York, that Lendal Bridge was built to link the city to the railway station. Today the river-boats carry tourists through the city and people stroll along the riverbanks.

LENDAL BRIDGE

The first Lendal Bridge, built of cast iron, collapsed with a spectacular crash which could be felt for miles around. The current bridge was designed by Thomas Page, who also designed Westminster Bridge in London. Lendal Tower predates the bridge: it was originally built as part of the city's defences and then, from 1616 until 1849, used as a water tower for pumping water into the city.

RIVER-BOAT CRUISE

The best view of the Guildhall is from Lendal Bridge or from the river. River cruises start from Lendal Bridge throughout the day and in the evening.

Lendal Bridge and Lendal Tower

Museum Gardens

The Museum Gardens include the ruins of St Mary's Abbey and were once part of the Abbey's grounds. They were laid out as a botanical garden by the Yorkshire Philosophical Society in the early 19th century. The plants and trees are carefully labelled and provide a splendid setting for the historic buildings which span York's history from the Romans to the 19th century.

HOSPITIUM

The Hospitium was built as a place where travellers to the Abbey could rest. The ground floor dates from about 1310 and the upper, timber-framed storey was added about a hundred years later, although it has since been restored several times.

ST OLAVE'S CHURCH

The original church was founded by Siward, the Danish Earl of Northumbria, in about 1050, but it was so badly damaged during the English Civil War that most of the present church dates from the 19th century. The artist William Etty is buried in the graveyard.

MUSEUM GARDENS

Museum Gardens is a popular place for local people as well as tourists to sit on the grass, feed the squirrels and watch the peacocks and the boats on the river.

OBSERVATORY

The octagonal Observatory, designed by John Smeaton for the Yorkshire Philosophical Society, was built in 1831. For many years it housed what was then the largest refracting telescope in the world.

Peacock in Museum Gardens

Museum Gardens

ST MARY'S ABBEY

St Mary's Abbey, founded in 1088 by a Benedictine monk from Whitby, was once the richest and most powerful abbey in northern England. The present ruins are of the abbey church which was rebuilt after a fire in the late 13th century. The Abbey, one of the most beautiful in England, was built outside the walls of the city and had its own precinct walls, which still remain along Marygate and Bootham. The Abbey was dissolved and plundered by Henry VIII's men in 1539, and much of its stone used to build the County Gaol and Ouse Bridge.

YORKSHIRE MUSEUM

The Yorkshire Museum building, designed by William Wilkins, who also designed the National Gallery in London, was opened in 1830. Part of the ruins of St Mary's Abbey are contained in the Museum as well as galleries depicting life in Roman times and archaeological items from the last 2,000 years, including the famous Middleham jewel, found at Middleham Castle, home of Richard III.

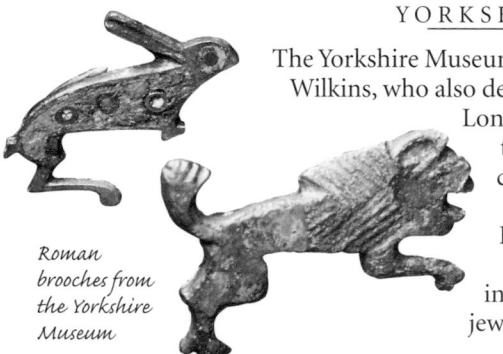

Roman brooches from the Yorkshire Museum

The Middleham jewel, a 15th-century pendant

MULTANGULAR TOWER

The ten-sided Multangular Tower is almost all that remains of the Roman walls. The base of the tower is 2 metres (6 feet) thick and the row of Roman tiles nearly 2.4 metres (8 feet) above the ground can be seen on the inside and outside of the tower. The upper 3.3 metres (11 feet) of stonework were added in medieval times, when the Tower still formed part of the city's defences.

Roman kitchen in the Yorkshire Museum

MONKS' DEPARTURE

In 1131 Cistercian monks founded their first religious house at Rievaulx (▷ 31), just north of York. Their strict religious life, which included hard physical labour, appealed to some of the monks at St Mary's Abbey, who felt that life in their Abbey had become too lax. When the abbot refused to reform St Mary's in 1132, a group of 13 monks, led by Prior Richard, left the Abbey and set up a new Cistercian house, Fountains Abbey, on the banks of the River Skell.

ST LEONARD'S HOSPITAL

St Leonard's Hospital once occupied a large part of what is now St Leonard's Place and Museum Street. It was originally attached to the Minster until it was suppressed by Henry VIII during the Reformation. Only parts of the vaulted undercroft, chapel and arched tunnel, the watergate to the river, now remain in the Museum Gardens and in the bar of the Theatre Royal.

St Leonard's Place

St Leonard's Place is a Regency terrace built over the site of the medieval St Leonard's Hospital. It links the Assembly Rooms and the Red House, two elegant Georgian mansions, with Exhibition Square and the City Art Gallery.

Assembly Rooms

ASSEMBLY ROOMS

In the 18th century York was the social capital of northern England. When the Assembly Rooms opened in 1732, wealthy and fashionable people from all over England flocked here, to meet, play cards and generally make a good impression. According to Daniel Defoe, 'A man converses here with all the world as effectually as at London.'

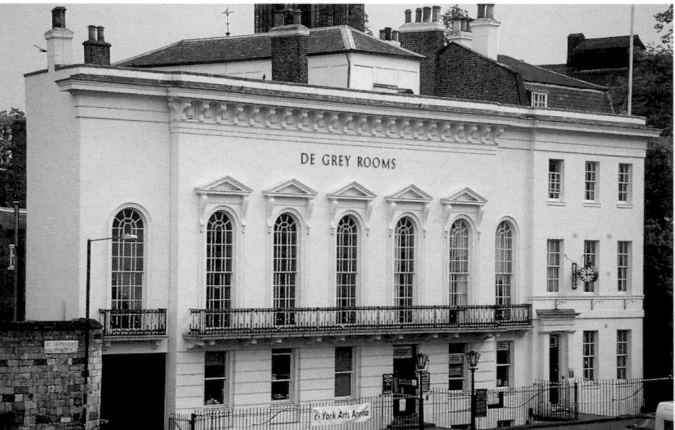

DE GREY ROOMS

The De Grey Rooms were designed in 1841 by G.T. Andrews, one of the architects of the terraced houses in St Leonard's Place, for concerts, balls and other entertainments as well as an officers' mess for the Yorkshire Hussars. This gracious building is still used for concerts and public meetings.

RED HOUSE

Many fine public and private buildings were erected in York in the first half of the 18th century. The Red House, built in 1714 by Sir William Robinson, the then Lord Mayor, was so elegant that his successor wanted to take it over as the Lord Mayor's house. Sir William refused and the Mansion House (▷20) was built in 1725.

Red House

LAURENCE STERNE (1713–68)

Born in Ireland, Laurence Sterne studied at Cambridge and became first a vicar and then prebend at York Minster, where he was known for preaching eccentric sermons. The first two volumes of his satirical novel 'Tristram Shandy' caused a sensation when they were published. The novel, published by a printer in Stonegate between 1759 and 1767, contains many characters based on local people. Sterne died in London in 1768.

ST LEONARD'S PLACE

One side of St Leonard's Place, which was built in 1844–45, is taken up with City of York Council offices. On the other side is the Theatre Royal, originally built in 1744 but later rebuilt and extended, and the De Grey Rooms.

CITY ART GALLERY

The York City Art Gallery has many world-famous paintings from Britain and Europe, including several works by the York artist William Etty (1787–1849). The Gallery also has an impressive collection of studio pottery.

Pottery by William Staite Murray in the York City Art Gallery

KING'S MANOR

Although St Mary's Abbey was reduced to ruins by Henry VIII, the Abbot's house survived and became King's Manor, the seat of the Council of the North until 1641. During the English Civil War, Charles I set up his headquarters in the building and it came under direct attack during the siege of the city in 1642. King's Manor was restored in 1964 and is now part of the University of York.

Coat of arms of Charles I

New wing of King's Manor

Historic Railways

The National Railway Museum, along Leeman Road behind the station, is the world's biggest railway museum, with 103 locomotives dating from the early years of rail travel to the present day, and 176 carriages and other rolling stock. It is particularly fitting that the museum should be in York, a major railway centre since the entrepreneur George Hudson brought the railways to the city in 1839.

ROAD TRAIN

A road train carries people from Duncombe Place near the Minster to the National Railway Museum. Between April and October, the train runs every half an hour.

The National Railway Museum

CHILDREN'S ACTIVITIES

Children as well as railway buffs enjoy the fascination of the locomotives and exhibits at the National Railway Museum. In addition, the museum has several areas and activities especially designed for children.

YORK RAILWAY STATION

York Station, designed by Thomas Prosser and opened in 1877, is a magnificent example of railway architecture. Slim Corinthian columns support the huge 244-metre (800-foot) curved roof on cast-iron rafters.

THE RAILWAY KING

The first train steamed into York in 1839 to a wooden platform in Queen Street, but George Hudson, recognising the potential of the railways, built a grander station, the forerunner of the present station. From here, he built up a railway empire that covered a quarter of the railway network and contributed greatly to York's commercial success in the 19th century. Hudson was Lord Mayor of York three times and a Member of Parliament before shady financial dealings came to light and he was disgraced.

'ROCKET'

Most people distrusted the noisy, fiery steam locomotives when they were first introduced, but after George Stephenson's 'Rocket' won the Rainhill Trials, a grand competition for locomotives in October 1829, people realised that railways had come to stay.

'MALLARD'

In July 1938 LNER's steam locomotive 'Mallard' pulled seven carriages down a track at just under 203 km/h (126 mph). It was just faster than a German 4-6-4 two years earlier and set a record that has never been broken by a steam locomotive.

MODEL RAILWAY MUSEUM

Beside the main station is the Model Railway Museum with several different scenes including one at night. The Intercity model travels 14 miles a day on these miniature tracks.

Out of Town Visits

York is within easy reach of many historic abbeys, stately homes and castles. Leeds, the spa town of Harrogate, and the Dales are a short train journey or drive away.

CASTLE HOWARD

Castle Howard, one of England's grandest houses, is just 15 miles from York, near Malton off the A64. This magnificent palace has been the family home of the Howards for 300 years and was used for the filming of 'Brideshead Revisited' from the novel by Evelyn Waugh. The 1,000 acres of parkland include a pyramid, boating lake, 400-year-old oak trees and one of the finest rose gardens in Europe.

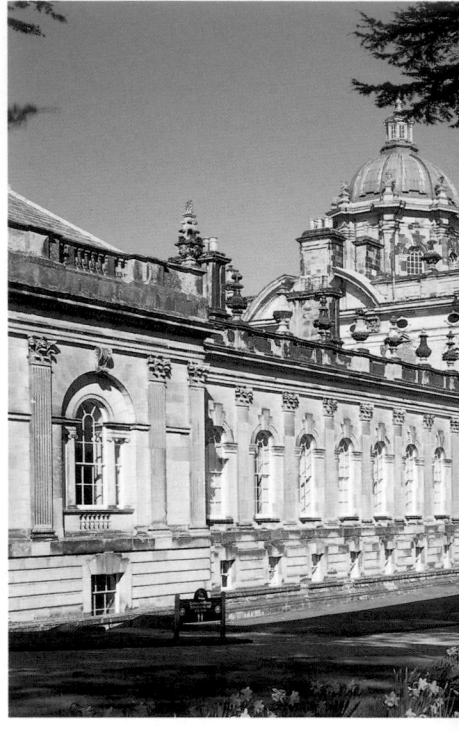

Helmsley Castle

HELMSLEY

The small, unspoilt town of Helmsley, just over 20 miles from York, is over-shadowed by a dramatic castle with keep and double earthworks.

THE WOLDS

This beautiful area of chalk down to the east of York stretches from Scarborough to Beverley. It is in sharp contrast to the bleakness of the North York Moors. Sledmere House off the A166 is a stately home with a famous stud farm, and is a good starting point to explore the Wolds.

Castle Howard

EDEN CAMP

Eden Camp is not just a museum of the Second World War but recreates what it was like to live through it. There are 27 huts, each concentrating on a particular theme, including a NAAFI canteen and an officers' mess.

Eden Camp

BENINGBROUGH HALL

Just eight miles north-west of York, Beningbrough Hall is an outstation of the National Portrait Gallery and includes 100 paintings by Gainsborough, Reynolds and Kneller. The house, designed by William Thornton in 1716 for John Bourchier, is an elegantly furnished Georgian house.

ALDBOROUGH ROMAN TOWN

Near Boroughbridge and about 20 miles north-west of York are the remains of a Roman town. The site includes mosaic pavements and city defences and a museum of Roman artifacts.

KNARESBOROUGH

Knaresborough, on the River Nidd, is just outside Harrogate and 22 miles from York. The 14th-century castle keep has an impressive dungeon and, below the high railway bridge across the Nidd, is Mother Shipton's Cave and the Dropping Well.

Pickering

PICKERING

Pickering, 26 miles north of York, is at one end of the North Yorkshire Moors Railway which steams across 18 miles of beautiful countryside to Grosmont. Pickering has a partly ruined medieval castle and a church with 15th-century wall frescoes to rival many in Italy.

RIEVAULX ABBEY

In 1131 a group of Cistercian monks was sent from Clairvaux in France to found the Order's first abbey in the north of England. Two miles from Helmsley, on the banks of the River Rye, the magnificent ruined arches emanate calm and tranquillity.

Rievaulx Abbey

City Plan

Lady Row, Goodramgate

TOURIST INFORMATION CENTRE
De Grey Rooms, St Leonard's Place
Exhibition Square, York YO1 7HB
telephone: 01904 621756
fax: 01904 625618
(Offices also at York Station
and in George Hudson Street)

SHOPMOBILITY
For the loan of manual or
electric wheelchairs and
powered scooters to anyone
who needs them.
Level 2, Piccadilly Car Park
(above C&A, Piccadilly)
telephone: 01904 679222

LOCAL BUS INFORMATION
telephone: 01904 551400

Micklegate Bar

TRIPS AND TOURS

Information of all of the following tours can be found at the Tourist Information Centre.

Walking tours: Guided walking tours include York-walk (01904 622303), the Complete York Tour (01904 706643) and several evening Ghost Walks.

Open-top buses: Guide Friday and other sightseeing tours can be joined at Exhibition Square and various places around York.

Boat trips: River cruises can be boarded at Lendal Bridge (also floodlit evening cruises) and at King's Staith. Or you can hire a self-drive motor boat. Phone York Boat (01904 623752) or York Marine (01904 704442).

Guided excursions: For trips to the Dales, the Moors and the coast, phone Eddie Brown Tours (01904 640760).

Guide Friday bus tour

Central York

Place of Interest		Public/Disabled Toilets
Place of Worship	+	Tourist Information Centre
Restricted Access		Car Park/Disabled
Shopping Street		Transport Station
One Way Street	→	View Point

This map is a simplified version of the Town & Heritage Map of York
Redrawn by The Map Studio, Romsey 1997, revised 2001
© George Philip Ltd, London, 1995

100   0   100
Metres   Yards